50 Legendary Seafood Recipes

By: Kelly Johnson

Table of Contents

- Lobster Newberg
- Shrimp Scampi
- Clam Chowder
- Paella
- Grilled Salmon with Lemon-Dill Sauce
- Crab Cakes
- Fish Tacos
- Seafood Paella
- Lobster Bisque
- Tuna Tartare
- Mussels in White Wine Sauce
- Scallops with Garlic Butter
- Shrimp and Grits
- Baked Cod with Herb Crust
- Shrimp Cocktail
- Oysters Rockefeller
- Fish and Chips
- Seafood Risotto
- Crab Stuffed Mushrooms
- Lobster Roll
- Grilled Octopus with Lemon
- Shrimp Alfredo
- Clams Casino
- Mahi Mahi with Mango Salsa
- Seafood Ceviche
- Grilled Swordfish Steaks
- Crab Louie Salad
- Shrimp and Lobster Ravioli
- Crab Bisque
- Tuna Steak with Avocado Salsa
- Fish Stew
- Lobster Mac and Cheese
- Sautéed Scallops with Asparagus
- Blackened Snapper
- Smoked Salmon Bagel

- Shrimp Tempura
- Salmon Croquettes
- Mussels Marinara
- Fried Catfish
- Grilled Shrimp Skewers
- Salmon Poke Bowl
- Scallop and Shrimp Skewers
- Lobster Tail with Garlic Butter
- Tuna Melt
- Clam Bake
- Fish Casserole
- Lobster Ravioli
- Shrimp and Spinach Salad
- Baked Tilapia with Lemon and Herbs
- Crab and Corn Chowder

Lobster Newberg

Ingredients:

- 2 lobster tails
- 3 large eggs
- 1/2 cup heavy cream
- 1/4 cup brandy (Cognac or sherry works well)
- 1 tablespoon butter
- 1 tablespoon lemon juice
- Salt and pepper to taste
- 1/4 cup crab meat (optional, for added richness)
- Fresh parsley for garnish

Instructions:

1. **Prepare the lobster tails:**
   Boil or steam the lobster tails until cooked through (about 5-7 minutes). Remove the lobster meat from the shells and chop into bite-sized pieces.
2. **Make the sauce:**
   In a double boiler, whisk together the eggs and heavy cream. Slowly heat, whisking constantly, until the mixture thickens. Stir in the brandy, butter, and lemon juice. Season with salt and pepper to taste.
3. **Combine lobster with the sauce:**
   Add the lobster meat (and crab meat, if using) to the sauce and stir to coat evenly.
4. **Serve:**
   Spoon the lobster mixture into serving dishes and garnish with fresh parsley. Serve immediately.

Shrimp Scampi

Ingredients:

- 1 lb large shrimp, peeled and deveined
- 4 cloves garlic, minced
- 1/2 cup white wine
- 1/2 cup chicken broth
- 1/4 cup butter
- 2 tablespoons olive oil
- Juice of 1 lemon
- 1/4 teaspoon red pepper flakes
- Salt and pepper to taste
- Fresh parsley, chopped
- Cooked pasta (spaghetti or linguine) for serving

Instructions:

1. **Cook the shrimp:**
   In a large skillet, heat olive oil and butter over medium heat. Add garlic and sauté for 1-2 minutes until fragrant. Add shrimp and cook for 2-3 minutes on each side, or until pink and cooked through. Remove shrimp and set aside.
2. **Make the sauce:**
   In the same skillet, add white wine, chicken broth, lemon juice, and red pepper flakes. Simmer for 2-3 minutes to reduce the sauce slightly.
3. **Combine shrimp and pasta:**
   Return the shrimp to the skillet, toss to coat in the sauce, and cook for another minute. Add cooked pasta to the skillet and toss to combine.
4. **Serve:**
   Season with salt and pepper to taste. Garnish with fresh parsley and serve immediately.

Clam Chowder

Ingredients:

- 2 cans (6.5 oz each) clams, drained and juice reserved
- 1 medium onion, chopped
- 2 stalks celery, chopped
- 2 medium potatoes, peeled and diced
- 2 cups chicken or vegetable broth
- 1 cup heavy cream
- 1/2 cup milk
- 1/4 cup butter
- 2 cloves garlic, minced
- Salt and pepper to taste
- Fresh parsley for garnish

Instructions:

1. **Cook the vegetables:**
   In a large pot, melt butter over medium heat. Add the onion, celery, and garlic, and sauté until softened, about 5 minutes.
2. **Add the potatoes and broth:**
   Add the diced potatoes and chicken broth to the pot. Bring to a boil, then reduce the heat and simmer until the potatoes are tender, about 10-15 minutes.
3. **Add the clams and cream:**
   Stir in the clams (with their juice), heavy cream, and milk. Cook for another 5-7 minutes to heat through. Season with salt and pepper to taste.
4. **Serve:**
   Garnish with fresh parsley and serve hot.

Paella

Ingredients:

- 1 lb chicken thighs, cut into pieces
- 1 lb shrimp, peeled and deveined
- 1/2 lb chorizo sausage, sliced
- 2 cups short-grain rice (Arborio or Bomba)
- 1 onion, chopped
- 2 cloves garlic, minced
- 1 red bell pepper, chopped
- 1 can (14.5 oz) diced tomatoes
- 4 cups chicken broth
- 1/4 teaspoon saffron threads
- 1/2 teaspoon paprika
- 1/4 teaspoon cayenne pepper
- 2 tablespoons olive oil
- Salt and pepper to taste
- Fresh parsley for garnish
- Lemon wedges for serving

Instructions:

1. **Prepare the ingredients:**
   Heat olive oil in a large paella pan or wide skillet over medium heat. Add the chicken and chorizo, and cook until browned. Remove and set aside.
2. **Cook the vegetables:**
   In the same pan, add the onion, garlic, and red bell pepper. Cook until softened, about 5 minutes. Add the diced tomatoes, saffron, paprika, and cayenne pepper.
3. **Add the rice and broth:**
   Stir in the rice, and add chicken broth. Bring to a boil, then reduce the heat and simmer for 15 minutes, stirring occasionally.
4. **Add the shrimp and chicken:**
   Return the chicken and chorizo to the pan. Add the shrimp on top and continue cooking until the rice is tender and the shrimp is pink, about 10 minutes.
5. **Serve:**
   Garnish with fresh parsley and lemon wedges. Serve immediately.

Grilled Salmon with Lemon-Dill Sauce

Ingredients:

- 4 salmon fillets
- 1 tablespoon olive oil
- Salt and pepper to taste
- 1/4 cup Greek yogurt
- 1 tablespoon mayonnaise
- 1 tablespoon lemon juice
- 1 teaspoon fresh dill, chopped
- Lemon wedges for serving

Instructions:

1. **Prepare the salmon:**
   Preheat the grill to medium-high heat. Brush the salmon fillets with olive oil and season with salt and pepper.
2. **Grill the salmon:**
   Grill the salmon for 4-5 minutes on each side, or until cooked through and flakes easily with a fork.
3. **Make the sauce:**
   In a small bowl, mix together Greek yogurt, mayonnaise, lemon juice, and dill. Season with salt and pepper.
4. **Serve:**
   Serve the grilled salmon with a dollop of lemon-dill sauce and lemon wedges on the side.

Crab Cakes

Ingredients:

- 1 lb fresh crab meat
- 1/4 cup breadcrumbs
- 2 tablespoons mayonnaise
- 1 egg
- 1 tablespoon Dijon mustard
- 1 tablespoon Worcestershire sauce
- 1 tablespoon lemon juice
- 1/4 teaspoon Old Bay seasoning
- 1 tablespoon parsley, chopped
- 2 tablespoons olive oil

Instructions:

1. **Prepare the crab mixture:**
   In a bowl, combine crab meat, breadcrumbs, mayonnaise, egg, mustard, Worcestershire sauce, lemon juice, Old Bay seasoning, and parsley. Mix gently until just combined.
2. **Form the cakes:**
   Shape the crab mixture into 6-8 patties, pressing lightly to hold them together.
3. **Cook the crab cakes:**
   Heat olive oil in a skillet over medium heat. Cook the crab cakes for 3-4 minutes on each side, until golden brown.
4. **Serve:**
   Serve hot with a side of tartar sauce or a squeeze of lemon.

Fish Tacos

Ingredients:

- 1 lb white fish fillets (tilapia, cod, or mahi-mahi)
- 1 tablespoon olive oil
- 1 teaspoon cumin
- 1 teaspoon paprika
- Salt and pepper to taste
- 8 small corn tortillas
- 1/2 cup shredded cabbage
- 1/4 cup cilantro, chopped
- 1/4 cup lime crema (Greek yogurt, lime juice, and a pinch of salt)

Instructions:

1. **Prepare the fish:**
   Preheat a skillet over medium heat. Season the fish fillets with olive oil, cumin, paprika, salt, and pepper. Cook the fish for 3-4 minutes on each side, until cooked through.
2. **Assemble the tacos:**
   Warm the tortillas and top with cooked fish, shredded cabbage, and cilantro. Drizzle with lime crema.
3. **Serve:**
   Serve immediately with extra lime wedges on the side.

Seafood Paella

Ingredients:

- 1 lb shrimp, peeled and deveined
- 1 lb mussels
- 1/2 lb squid, sliced into rings
- 1 onion, chopped
- 2 cloves garlic, minced
- 1 bell pepper, chopped
- 2 cups Arborio rice
- 1/4 teaspoon saffron threads
- 4 cups seafood stock
- 1/2 cup white wine
- 2 tablespoons olive oil
- Salt and pepper to taste
- Lemon wedges for serving

Instructions:

1. **Prepare the seafood:**
   In a paella pan, heat olive oil over medium heat. Add shrimp, mussels, and squid, cooking until shrimp turns pink. Remove and set aside.
2. **Cook the vegetables:**
   Add onion, garlic, and bell pepper to the pan, cooking until softened. Stir in the rice and saffron.
3. **Add the stock and wine:**
   Pour in the seafood stock and white wine, and simmer for 15-20 minutes until the rice is cooked.
4. **Combine the seafood:**
   Return the seafood to the pan and cook for another 5 minutes until everything is heated through.
5. **Serve:**
   Garnish with lemon wedges and serve hot.

Lobster Bisque

Ingredients:

- 2 lobster tails, cooked and chopped
- 2 tablespoons butter
- 1 small onion, chopped
- 2 cloves garlic, minced
- 1/2 cup dry white wine
- 2 cups lobster stock
- 1/2 cup heavy cream
- 1 tablespoon tomato paste
- 1/4 teaspoon paprika
- Salt and pepper to taste
- Fresh parsley for garnish

Instructions:

1. **Make the base:**
   In a large pot, melt butter over medium heat. Add onion and garlic, cooking until softened. Add white wine, lobster stock, tomato paste, paprika, salt, and pepper. Simmer for 10 minutes.
2. **Puree the soup:**
   Use an immersion blender to puree the soup until smooth, or transfer to a blender. Return to the pot.
3. **Add the lobster:**
   Stir in the chopped lobster meat and heavy cream. Cook for another 5 minutes, then season with additional salt and pepper.
4. **Serve:**
   Garnish with parsley and serve hot.

Tuna Tartare

Ingredients:

- 1 lb sushi-grade tuna, finely diced
- 1/4 cup soy sauce
- 1 tablespoon sesame oil
- 1 teaspoon rice vinegar
- 1 tablespoon Dijon mustard
- 1/4 teaspoon grated ginger
- 1/4 cup green onions, finely chopped
- 1 tablespoon toasted sesame seeds
- 1/2 avocado, diced (optional)
- Fresh cilantro for garnish

Instructions:

1. **Prepare the tuna:**
   Place the finely diced tuna in a bowl.
2. **Make the dressing:**
   In a small bowl, whisk together the soy sauce, sesame oil, rice vinegar, Dijon mustard, and grated ginger.
3. **Combine:**
   Pour the dressing over the tuna and toss gently to coat. Add green onions, sesame seeds, and diced avocado (if using). Toss again.
4. **Serve:**
   Spoon the tartare into serving bowls and garnish with fresh cilantro. Serve immediately with crackers or thinly sliced baguette.

Mussels in White Wine Sauce

Ingredients:

- 2 lbs mussels, cleaned and debearded
- 2 tablespoons butter
- 1 tablespoon olive oil
- 1 small onion, finely chopped
- 4 cloves garlic, minced
- 1/2 cup white wine
- 1/4 cup heavy cream
- 1 tablespoon fresh parsley, chopped
- Salt and pepper to taste
- Lemon wedges for serving

Instructions:

1. **Sauté the vegetables:**
   In a large pot, heat olive oil and butter over medium heat. Add onion and garlic, and sauté until softened, about 3-4 minutes.
2. **Cook the mussels:**
   Add the mussels to the pot and pour in the white wine. Cover the pot and cook for about 5-7 minutes, or until the mussels open.
3. **Finish the sauce:**
   Discard any unopened mussels. Stir in heavy cream and season with salt and pepper. Cook for an additional 2 minutes.
4. **Serve:**
   Garnish with fresh parsley and lemon wedges. Serve immediately with crusty bread to soak up the sauce.

Scallops with Garlic Butter

Ingredients:

- 1 lb sea scallops, patted dry
- 2 tablespoons butter
- 2 tablespoons olive oil
- 3 cloves garlic, minced
- 1 tablespoon lemon juice
- 1/4 teaspoon red pepper flakes (optional)
- Salt and pepper to taste
- Fresh parsley, chopped for garnish

Instructions:

1. **Cook the scallops:**
   Heat olive oil and butter in a large skillet over medium-high heat. Once hot, add the scallops and cook for 2-3 minutes on each side, until golden brown and cooked through. Remove scallops and set aside.
2. **Make the garlic butter:**
   In the same skillet, add garlic and sauté for 1 minute until fragrant. Add lemon juice, red pepper flakes (if using), and season with salt and pepper.
3. **Combine and serve:**
   Return the scallops to the skillet and toss in the garlic butter. Garnish with fresh parsley and serve immediately.

Shrimp and Grits

Ingredients:

- 1 lb shrimp, peeled and deveined
- 1 cup grits (stone-ground)
- 4 cups water or chicken broth
- 1/4 cup heavy cream
- 1/4 cup cheddar cheese, shredded
- 1 tablespoon butter
- 4 slices bacon, chopped
- 1/2 small onion, chopped
- 2 cloves garlic, minced
- 1/2 teaspoon paprika
- Salt and pepper to taste
- Fresh parsley for garnish

Instructions:

1. **Prepare the grits:**
   Bring the water or broth to a boil in a medium saucepan. Stir in the grits and cook according to package instructions, about 20-25 minutes. Once cooked, stir in the heavy cream, cheddar cheese, and butter. Season with salt and pepper.
2. **Cook the shrimp:**
   In a large skillet, cook the bacon until crispy. Remove the bacon and set aside. Add the onion and garlic to the skillet and sauté until softened. Add the shrimp, paprika, salt, and pepper, and cook for 3-4 minutes until pink and cooked through.
3. **Serve:**
   Spoon the grits onto plates, top with shrimp and bacon, and garnish with fresh parsley. Serve immediately.

Baked Cod with Herb Crust

Ingredients:

- 4 cod fillets
- 1/4 cup breadcrumbs
- 2 tablespoons fresh parsley, chopped
- 2 tablespoons fresh basil, chopped
- 1 tablespoon fresh thyme, chopped
- 2 tablespoons olive oil
- 1 tablespoon lemon juice
- Salt and pepper to taste
- Lemon wedges for serving

Instructions:

1. **Prepare the crust:**
   In a small bowl, combine breadcrumbs, parsley, basil, thyme, olive oil, lemon juice, salt, and pepper.
2. **Prepare the cod:**
   Preheat the oven to 400°F (200°C). Place the cod fillets on a baking sheet lined with parchment paper. Season with salt and pepper.
3. **Add the crust:**
   Spoon the breadcrumb mixture over each fillet, pressing gently to adhere.
4. **Bake the cod:**
   Bake the cod for 12-15 minutes, or until the fish flakes easily with a fork.
5. **Serve:**
   Garnish with lemon wedges and serve immediately.

Shrimp Cocktail

Ingredients:

- 1 lb large shrimp, peeled and deveined, tails on
- 1 tablespoon salt
- 1 lemon, sliced
- 1 tablespoon black peppercorns
- 1/2 cup cocktail sauce

Instructions:

1. **Prepare the shrimp:**
   In a large pot, bring water to a boil and add salt, lemon slices, and peppercorns. Add the shrimp and cook for 2-3 minutes until they turn pink.
2. **Chill the shrimp:**
   Remove the shrimp from the pot and transfer them to a bowl of ice water to cool. Drain once chilled.
3. **Serve:**
   Arrange the shrimp on a platter and serve with cocktail sauce for dipping.

Oysters Rockefeller

Ingredients:

- 12 oysters, on the half shell
- 1 tablespoon butter
- 2 cloves garlic, minced
- 1/2 cup spinach, chopped
- 1/4 cup breadcrumbs
- 1/4 cup grated Parmesan cheese
- 1 tablespoon Pernod (optional)
- Salt and pepper to taste
- Lemon wedges for serving

Instructions:

1. **Prepare the spinach:**
   In a skillet, melt butter over medium heat. Add garlic and cook for 1 minute. Stir in spinach and cook until wilted. Season with salt and pepper. Remove from heat.
2. **Prepare the oysters:**
   Preheat the broiler. Place the oysters on a baking sheet. Spoon the spinach mixture onto each oyster, then top with breadcrumbs and Parmesan cheese.
3. **Broil the oysters:**
   Broil the oysters for 3-4 minutes, until the topping is golden brown.
4. **Serve:**
   Garnish with lemon wedges and serve immediately.

Fish and Chips

Ingredients:

- 4 white fish fillets (cod, haddock, or tilapia)
- 1 cup all-purpose flour
- 1 tablespoon baking powder
- 1 teaspoon salt
- 1 teaspoon paprika
- 1 cup cold beer
- 1/2 cup cornstarch
- Vegetable oil for frying
- 2 large potatoes, peeled and cut into fries
- Malt vinegar for serving

Instructions:

1. **Prepare the fries:**
   Heat vegetable oil in a deep fryer or large pot to 350°F (175°C). Fry the potato fries until golden brown and crispy, about 4-5 minutes. Remove and drain on paper towels.
2. **Make the batter:**
   In a bowl, combine flour, baking powder, salt, paprika, and cold beer. Whisk until smooth.
3. **Fry the fish:**
   Dip the fish fillets into the batter and carefully lower them into the hot oil. Fry for 4-5 minutes until golden brown. Remove and drain on paper towels.
4. **Serve:**
   Serve the fish and chips with malt vinegar on the side.

Seafood Risotto

Ingredients:

- 1 lb mixed seafood (shrimp, scallops, mussels, or squid)
- 1 1/2 cups Arborio rice
- 4 cups seafood broth
- 1/2 cup dry white wine
- 1/2 cup grated Parmesan cheese
- 1/4 cup butter
- 1/2 onion, chopped
- 2 cloves garlic, minced
- Salt and pepper to taste
- Fresh parsley for garnish

Instructions:

1. **Sauté the onions and garlic:**
   In a large pan, melt butter over medium heat. Add onion and garlic, and sauté until softened.
2. **Cook the rice:**
   Stir in the Arborio rice and cook for 2 minutes until lightly toasted. Add white wine and cook until the wine is absorbed.
3. **Add the broth:**
   Gradually add seafood broth, one ladle at a time, stirring constantly and allowing each addition to absorb before adding the next. Continue until the rice is tender and creamy, about 18-20 minutes.
4. **Add the seafood:**
   Stir in the mixed seafood and cook for 3-4 minutes until heated through. Stir in Parmesan cheese and season with salt and pepper.
5. **Serve:**
   Garnish with fresh parsley and serve immediately.

Crab Stuffed Mushrooms

Ingredients:

- 12 large mushroom caps, cleaned and stems removed
- 8 oz crab meat, cooked and flaked
- 1/4 cup cream cheese, softened
- 2 tablespoons mayonnaise
- 1 tablespoon Dijon mustard
- 1 tablespoon fresh parsley, chopped
- 1/2 cup breadcrumbs
- 1/4 cup Parmesan cheese, grated
- 1 tablespoon lemon juice
- Salt and pepper to taste
- Olive oil for drizzling

Instructions:

1. **Prepare the filling:**
   In a bowl, combine crab meat, cream cheese, mayonnaise, Dijon mustard, parsley, breadcrumbs, Parmesan cheese, lemon juice, salt, and pepper. Mix until well combined.
2. **Stuff the mushrooms:**
   Spoon the crab mixture into the mushroom caps, pressing gently to pack the filling.
3. **Bake the mushrooms:**
   Preheat the oven to 375°F (190°C). Place the stuffed mushrooms on a baking sheet, drizzle with olive oil, and bake for 15-20 minutes, or until golden brown and bubbly.
4. **Serve:**
   Serve hot as an appetizer or side dish.

Lobster Roll

Ingredients:

- 2 lobster tails, cooked and chopped
- 1/4 cup mayonnaise
- 1 tablespoon fresh lemon juice
- 1 teaspoon Dijon mustard
- 1/4 teaspoon Old Bay seasoning
- 2 brioche rolls or hot dog buns, split and lightly toasted
- Fresh parsley for garnish
- Salt and pepper to taste

Instructions:

1. **Prepare the lobster salad:**
   In a bowl, combine the chopped lobster, mayonnaise, lemon juice, Dijon mustard, Old Bay seasoning, salt, and pepper. Mix until well combined.
2. **Assemble the rolls:**
   Spoon the lobster mixture into the toasted rolls.
3. **Serve:**
   Garnish with fresh parsley and serve immediately.

Grilled Octopus with Lemon

Ingredients:

- 2 lbs octopus, cleaned
- 3 tablespoons olive oil
- 2 cloves garlic, minced
- 1 tablespoon fresh lemon juice
- 1 teaspoon dried oregano
- Salt and pepper to taste
- Lemon wedges for serving

Instructions:

1. **Prepare the octopus:**
   Bring a large pot of salted water to a boil. Add the octopus and simmer for about 45 minutes until tender. Remove and let it cool.
2. **Grill the octopus:**
   Preheat the grill to medium-high heat. Cut the octopus into smaller pieces (tentacles and body). Toss the octopus pieces with olive oil, garlic, lemon juice, oregano, salt, and pepper.
3. **Grill the octopus:**
   Grill the octopus for 2-3 minutes on each side until lightly charred.
4. **Serve:**
   Serve with lemon wedges and enjoy immediately.

Shrimp Alfredo

Ingredients:

- 1 lb shrimp, peeled and deveined
- 8 oz fettuccine pasta
- 2 tablespoons butter
- 2 cloves garlic, minced
- 1 cup heavy cream
- 1/2 cup grated Parmesan cheese
- Salt and pepper to taste
- Fresh parsley for garnish

Instructions:

1. **Cook the pasta:**
   Cook the fettuccine according to package instructions. Drain and set aside.
2. **Cook the shrimp:**
   In a large skillet, melt the butter over medium heat. Add garlic and sauté for 1 minute. Add the shrimp, season with salt and pepper, and cook for 3-4 minutes, until pink and cooked through.
3. **Make the Alfredo sauce:**
   Add the heavy cream to the skillet and bring to a simmer. Stir in the Parmesan cheese and cook until the sauce thickens, about 2-3 minutes.
4. **Combine the pasta and shrimp:**
   Add the cooked pasta to the skillet and toss to coat with the Alfredo sauce.
5. **Serve:**
   Garnish with fresh parsley and serve immediately.

Clams Casino

Ingredients:

- 12 fresh clams, shucked
- 1/2 cup breadcrumbs
- 1/4 cup grated Parmesan cheese
- 2 tablespoons butter, melted
- 2 cloves garlic, minced
- 1/4 teaspoon paprika
- 2 tablespoons fresh parsley, chopped
- Lemon wedges for serving

Instructions:

1. **Prepare the clams:**
   Preheat the oven to 375°F (190°C). Place the shucked clams on a baking sheet.
2. **Make the topping:**
   In a small bowl, combine the breadcrumbs, Parmesan cheese, melted butter, garlic, paprika, and parsley.
3. **Stuff the clams:**
   Spoon the breadcrumb mixture onto each clam.
4. **Bake the clams:**
   Bake for 10-12 minutes, or until the topping is golden and crispy.
5. **Serve:**
   Serve with lemon wedges.

Mahi Mahi with Mango Salsa

Ingredients:

- 4 mahi mahi fillets
- 1 tablespoon olive oil
- Salt and pepper to taste
- 1 mango, peeled and diced
- 1/4 cup red onion, finely chopped
- 1/4 cup fresh cilantro, chopped
- 1 tablespoon lime juice

Instructions:

1. **Cook the mahi mahi:**
   Preheat the grill or a skillet over medium-high heat. Drizzle the mahi mahi fillets with olive oil and season with salt and pepper. Cook for 4-5 minutes on each side, until golden and cooked through.
2. **Make the mango salsa:**
   In a bowl, combine the diced mango, red onion, cilantro, and lime juice. Stir gently.
3. **Serve:**
   Top the grilled mahi mahi with the mango salsa and serve immediately.

Seafood Ceviche

Ingredients:

- 1/2 lb shrimp, peeled and deveined
- 1/2 lb scallops, diced
- 1/2 lb white fish fillets, diced (such as tilapia)
- 1/2 cup lime juice
- 1/4 cup lemon juice
- 1/2 red onion, finely chopped
- 1/2 cucumber, diced
- 1/2 avocado, diced
- 1/4 cup cilantro, chopped
- Salt and pepper to taste

Instructions:

1. **Prepare the seafood:**
   In a bowl, combine the shrimp, scallops, and fish. Pour the lime and lemon juice over the seafood, ensuring it's well-covered. Let it marinate for 2-3 hours in the refrigerator, until the seafood is "cooked" through (it will turn opaque).
2. **Add the vegetables:**
   Stir in the red onion, cucumber, avocado, and cilantro. Season with salt and pepper to taste.
3. **Serve:**
   Serve chilled as an appetizer with tortilla chips or on its own.

Grilled Swordfish Steaks

Ingredients:

- 4 swordfish steaks
- 2 tablespoons olive oil
- 2 cloves garlic, minced
- 1 tablespoon lemon juice
- 1 teaspoon dried oregano
- Salt and pepper to taste
- Lemon wedges for serving

Instructions:

1. **Prepare the marinade:**
   In a small bowl, whisk together olive oil, garlic, lemon juice, oregano, salt, and pepper.
2. **Marinate the swordfish:**
   Place the swordfish steaks in a shallow dish and pour the marinade over them. Let them marinate for 30 minutes.
3. **Grill the swordfish:**
   Preheat the grill to medium-high heat. Grill the swordfish for 4-5 minutes on each side, or until cooked through and grill marks appear.
4. **Serve:**
   Serve with lemon wedges and enjoy immediately.

Crab Louie Salad

Ingredients:

- 1 lb crab meat (preferably fresh or lump)
- 4 cups mixed greens (such as arugula, spinach, or romaine)
- 2 tomatoes, sliced
- 1 avocado, sliced
- 2 hard-boiled eggs, quartered
- 1/4 cup red onion, thinly sliced
- 1/2 cucumber, sliced
- 1/4 cup green onions, chopped
- 1 tablespoon fresh parsley, chopped

For the Dressing:

- 1/2 cup mayonnaise
- 1 tablespoon ketchup
- 1 tablespoon Dijon mustard
- 1 tablespoon Worcestershire sauce
- 1 teaspoon hot sauce
- 1 teaspoon lemon juice
- Salt and pepper to taste

Instructions:

1. **Make the dressing:**
   In a bowl, whisk together the mayonnaise, ketchup, Dijon mustard, Worcestershire sauce, hot sauce, lemon juice, salt, and pepper until smooth. Adjust seasoning to taste.
2. **Prepare the salad:**
   Arrange the mixed greens, sliced tomatoes, avocado, hard-boiled eggs, red onion, cucumber, and green onions on a large plate or salad bowl.
3. **Top with crab:**
   Gently toss the crab meat with a little of the dressing to coat it. Spoon the crab mixture over the salad.
4. **Serve:**
   Drizzle the remaining dressing over the salad, garnish with fresh parsley, and serve immediately.

Shrimp and Lobster Ravioli

Ingredients:

- 1/2 lb lobster meat, chopped
- 1/2 lb shrimp, peeled, deveined, and chopped
- 1/2 cup ricotta cheese
- 1/4 cup Parmesan cheese, grated
- 1 tablespoon fresh parsley, chopped
- 1 egg (for binding)
- 1 package fresh or frozen ravioli wrappers
- 1/2 cup butter
- 2 cloves garlic, minced
- 1/4 cup dry white wine
- Salt and pepper to taste

Instructions:

1. **Prepare the filling:**
   In a bowl, combine the lobster meat, shrimp, ricotta, Parmesan, parsley, and egg. Season with salt and pepper and mix until smooth.
2. **Stuff the ravioli:**
   Place a small spoonful of the filling in the center of each ravioli wrapper. Moisten the edges with a little water, fold the wrappers over, and seal the edges.
3. **Cook the ravioli:**
   Bring a large pot of salted water to a boil. Drop the ravioli in batches into the water and cook for 3-4 minutes, or until they float to the top.
4. **Make the sauce:**
   In a skillet, melt the butter over medium heat. Add the garlic and sauté for 1-2 minutes. Add the white wine and cook for 2-3 minutes, until slightly reduced.
5. **Serve:**
   Add the cooked ravioli to the skillet and toss gently to coat in the sauce. Serve immediately.

Crab Bisque

Ingredients:

- 1 lb crab meat
- 2 tablespoons butter
- 1 onion, chopped
- 2 cloves garlic, minced
- 1 carrot, diced
- 2 celery stalks, diced
- 1/4 cup flour
- 4 cups chicken broth
- 1 cup heavy cream
- 1/2 teaspoon Old Bay seasoning
- 1/4 teaspoon cayenne pepper (optional)
- Salt and pepper to taste
- Fresh parsley for garnish

Instructions:

1. **Cook the vegetables:**
   In a large pot, melt the butter over medium heat. Add the onion, garlic, carrot, and celery. Sauté for 5-7 minutes, until softened.
2. **Make the roux:**
   Sprinkle the flour over the vegetables and cook for 2 minutes, stirring constantly.
3. **Add the broth and cream:**
   Gradually whisk in the chicken broth, making sure to avoid lumps. Bring to a simmer and cook for 10 minutes.
4. **Add the crab and seasoning:**
   Stir in the crab meat, heavy cream, Old Bay seasoning, cayenne pepper, salt, and pepper. Simmer for an additional 5-7 minutes.
5. **Serve:**
   Garnish with fresh parsley and serve hot.

Tuna Steak with Avocado Salsa

Ingredients:

- 2 tuna steaks
- 1 tablespoon olive oil
- Salt and pepper to taste
- 1 avocado, diced
- 1/2 red onion, finely chopped
- 1 small tomato, diced
- 1 tablespoon cilantro, chopped
- 1 tablespoon lime juice

Instructions:

1. **Cook the tuna steaks:**
   Heat the olive oil in a skillet over medium-high heat. Season the tuna steaks with salt and pepper. Sear the tuna steaks for 2-3 minutes on each side for medium-rare, or longer if desired.
2. **Make the avocado salsa:**
   In a bowl, combine the avocado, red onion, tomato, cilantro, and lime juice. Season with salt and pepper.
3. **Serve:**
   Top the cooked tuna steaks with the avocado salsa and serve immediately.

Fish Stew

Ingredients:

- 1 lb white fish fillets (such as cod or tilapia), cut into chunks
- 1 tablespoon olive oil
- 1 onion, chopped
- 2 cloves garlic, minced
- 1 can (14 oz) diced tomatoes
- 2 cups fish stock
- 1 cup dry white wine
- 2 potatoes, diced
- 1 teaspoon paprika
- 1/2 teaspoon thyme
- Salt and pepper to taste
- Fresh parsley for garnish

Instructions:

1. **Cook the aromatics:**
   Heat olive oil in a large pot over medium heat. Add the onion and garlic, cooking until softened.
2. **Add the vegetables and liquids:**
   Add the diced potatoes, tomatoes, fish stock, white wine, paprika, and thyme. Bring to a simmer and cook for 15-20 minutes, or until the potatoes are tender.
3. **Add the fish:**
   Add the fish chunks to the pot and cook for 5-7 minutes, until the fish is cooked through.
4. **Serve:**
   Season with salt and pepper to taste. Garnish with fresh parsley and serve hot.

Lobster Mac and Cheese

Ingredients:

- 2 cups cooked lobster meat, chopped
- 8 oz elbow macaroni
- 2 tablespoons butter
- 2 tablespoons flour
- 2 cups milk
- 1 cup shredded cheddar cheese
- 1/2 cup Parmesan cheese, grated
- 1/4 teaspoon garlic powder
- Salt and pepper to taste
- 1/4 cup breadcrumbs (optional)

Instructions:

1. **Cook the macaroni:**
   Cook the macaroni according to package instructions. Drain and set aside.
2. **Make the cheese sauce:**
   In a saucepan, melt the butter over medium heat. Stir in the flour and cook for 1-2 minutes. Gradually whisk in the milk and cook until thickened. Stir in the cheddar cheese, Parmesan, garlic powder, salt, and pepper.
3. **Combine with lobster and macaroni:**
   Stir the lobster meat and cooked macaroni into the cheese sauce.
4. **Serve:**
   If desired, top with breadcrumbs and bake at 350°F (175°C) for 15 minutes, or serve immediately as is.

Sautéed Scallops with Asparagus

Ingredients:

- 12 large scallops, cleaned
- 1 tablespoon olive oil
- 1 bunch asparagus, trimmed and cut into 2-inch pieces
- 2 cloves garlic, minced
- 1/2 cup white wine
- 1 tablespoon fresh lemon juice
- Salt and pepper to taste
- Fresh parsley for garnish

Instructions:

1. **Sauté the scallops:**
   Heat olive oil in a large skillet over medium-high heat. Season the scallops with salt and pepper and cook for 2-3 minutes per side until golden brown and cooked through. Remove and set aside.
2. **Cook the asparagus:**
   In the same skillet, add the asparagus and garlic. Sauté for 3-4 minutes until the asparagus is tender.
3. **Make the sauce:**
   Add white wine and lemon juice to the skillet, scraping up any brown bits from the bottom of the pan. Cook for 2-3 minutes until the sauce reduces slightly.
4. **Serve:**
   Return the scallops to the skillet, toss to combine, and serve with fresh parsley.

Blackened Snapper

Ingredients:

- 2 snapper fillets
- 2 tablespoons olive oil
- 1 tablespoon paprika
- 1 teaspoon cayenne pepper
- 1 teaspoon garlic powder
- 1/2 teaspoon onion powder
- Salt and pepper to taste
- Lemon wedges for serving

Instructions:

1. **Prepare the seasoning:**
   In a small bowl, mix paprika, cayenne pepper, garlic powder, onion powder, salt, and pepper.
2. **Season the snapper:**
   Rub both sides of the snapper fillets with the seasoning mixture.
3. **Cook the snapper:**
   Heat olive oil in a skillet over medium-high heat. Cook the snapper for 3-4 minutes per side until crispy and cooked through.
4. **Serve:**
   Serve the snapper with lemon wedges.

Smoked Salmon Bagel

Ingredients:

- 2 bagels, sliced and toasted
- 4 oz smoked salmon
- 2 tablespoons cream cheese
- 1 tablespoon fresh dill, chopped
- 1/2 red onion, thinly sliced
- 1 tablespoon capers (optional)
- Lemon wedges for serving

Instructions:

1. **Assemble the bagels:**
   Spread cream cheese on each toasted bagel half.
2. **Top with smoked salmon:**
   Layer the smoked salmon, red onion, dill, and capers on top of the cream cheese.
3. **Serve:**
   Serve with lemon wedges on the side.

Shrimp Tempura

Ingredients:

- 1 lb large shrimp, peeled and deveined
- 1 cup all-purpose flour
- 1/4 cup cornstarch
- 1 teaspoon baking powder
- 1 teaspoon salt
- 1 cup ice-cold sparkling water (or cold water)
- 1/2 teaspoon paprika (optional)
- Vegetable oil for frying

For the dipping sauce:

- 1/4 cup soy sauce
- 2 tablespoons rice vinegar
- 1 teaspoon sugar
- 1 teaspoon grated ginger

Instructions:

1. **Prepare the shrimp:**
   Pat the shrimp dry with paper towels. Set aside.
2. **Make the batter:**
   In a large bowl, whisk together the flour, cornstarch, baking powder, salt, and paprika. Gradually add the ice-cold sparkling water, mixing until the batter is smooth but slightly lumpy.
3. **Heat the oil:**
   In a deep fryer or large pot, heat the vegetable oil to 350°F (175°C).
4. **Coat the shrimp:**
   Dip each shrimp into the batter, allowing any excess to drip off. Carefully place the shrimp in the hot oil, frying in batches for 2-3 minutes or until golden and crispy. Remove and drain on paper towels.
5. **Make the dipping sauce:**
   Combine the soy sauce, rice vinegar, sugar, and ginger in a small bowl, stirring until the sugar dissolves.
6. **Serve:**
   Serve the shrimp tempura hot with the dipping sauce on the side.

Salmon Croquettes

Ingredients:

- 1 lb cooked salmon, flaked
- 1/2 cup breadcrumbs
- 1/4 cup mayonnaise
- 1/4 cup green onions, chopped
- 1 tablespoon Dijon mustard
- 1 egg
- 1/2 teaspoon paprika
- 1/4 teaspoon garlic powder
- Salt and pepper to taste
- 1 tablespoon olive oil (for frying)

Instructions:

1. **Make the croquette mixture:**
   In a bowl, combine the flaked salmon, breadcrumbs, mayonnaise, green onions, Dijon mustard, egg, paprika, garlic powder, salt, and pepper. Mix until well combined.
2. **Form the croquettes:**
   Shape the mixture into small patties or croquettes, about 2-3 inches in diameter.
3. **Fry the croquettes:**
   Heat olive oil in a large skillet over medium heat. Fry the croquettes for 3-4 minutes per side, until golden brown and crispy.
4. **Serve:**
   Serve the salmon croquettes with a squeeze of lemon or a dipping sauce of your choice.

Mussels Marinara

Ingredients:

- 2 lbs fresh mussels, cleaned and debearded
- 2 tablespoons olive oil
- 4 cloves garlic, minced
- 1 can (14 oz) crushed tomatoes
- 1 teaspoon red pepper flakes (optional)
- 1/2 cup dry white wine
- 1/4 cup fresh parsley, chopped
- Salt and pepper to taste

Instructions:

1. **Cook the garlic:**
   Heat olive oil in a large skillet over medium heat. Add the garlic and red pepper flakes, cooking for 1 minute until fragrant.
2. **Add the tomatoes and wine:**
   Stir in the crushed tomatoes and white wine. Simmer for 10-15 minutes, allowing the sauce to reduce slightly.
3. **Add the mussels:**
   Add the mussels to the skillet, cover, and cook for 5-7 minutes, shaking the skillet occasionally, until the mussels open.
4. **Finish the dish:**
   Discard any mussels that do not open. Season with salt and pepper and stir in fresh parsley.
5. **Serve:**
   Serve the mussels marinara with crusty bread for dipping.

Fried Catfish

Ingredients:

- 1 lb catfish fillets
- 1 cup cornmeal
- 1/2 cup flour
- 1 teaspoon paprika
- 1 teaspoon garlic powder
- 1/2 teaspoon cayenne pepper (optional)
- Salt and pepper to taste
- 1 egg
- 1/4 cup buttermilk
- Vegetable oil for frying

Instructions:

1. **Prepare the coating:**
   In a shallow bowl, combine cornmeal, flour, paprika, garlic powder, cayenne pepper, salt, and pepper.
2. **Prepare the catfish:**
   In another bowl, whisk together the egg and buttermilk.
3. **Coat the catfish:**
   Dip each fillet into the egg mixture, then coat it with the cornmeal mixture, pressing gently to adhere.
4. **Fry the catfish:**
   Heat vegetable oil in a large skillet over medium-high heat. Fry the catfish fillets for 4-5 minutes per side until golden brown and crispy.
5. **Serve:**
   Serve the fried catfish with lemon wedges and tartar sauce.

Grilled Shrimp Skewers

Ingredients:

- 1 lb large shrimp, peeled and deveined
- 1 tablespoon olive oil
- 2 tablespoons lemon juice
- 2 garlic cloves, minced
- 1 teaspoon paprika
- 1/2 teaspoon cayenne pepper (optional)
- Salt and pepper to taste
- Wooden skewers (soaked in water for 30 minutes)

Instructions:

1. **Marinate the shrimp:**
   In a bowl, combine olive oil, lemon juice, garlic, paprika, cayenne, salt, and pepper. Add the shrimp and toss to coat. Let marinate for 15-20 minutes.
2. **Prepare the skewers:**
   Thread the marinated shrimp onto the skewers.
3. **Grill the shrimp:**
   Preheat the grill to medium-high heat. Grill the shrimp for 2-3 minutes per side, or until they turn pink and opaque.
4. **Serve:**
   Serve the grilled shrimp skewers with extra lemon wedges and your favorite dipping sauce.

Salmon Poke Bowl

Ingredients:

- 1 lb fresh sushi-grade salmon, diced
- 2 cups cooked white or brown rice
- 1/4 cup soy sauce
- 1 tablespoon sesame oil
- 1 tablespoon rice vinegar
- 1 teaspoon honey
- 1/2 avocado, sliced
- 1/4 cucumber, thinly sliced
- 1/4 cup edamame (optional)
- 1 tablespoon sesame seeds
- 1 tablespoon green onions, chopped

Instructions:

1. **Prepare the poke bowl:**
   In a bowl, combine the diced salmon with soy sauce, sesame oil, rice vinegar, and honey. Stir gently to coat the salmon.
2. **Assemble the bowl:**
   Spoon the cooked rice into bowls. Top with the marinated salmon, avocado, cucumber, edamame, and any other desired toppings.
3. **Finish the dish:**
   Sprinkle sesame seeds and chopped green onions over the top.
4. **Serve:**
   Serve the poke bowl immediately with extra soy sauce or sriracha on the side.

Scallop and Shrimp Skewers

Ingredients:

- 8 large scallops
- 8 large shrimp, peeled and deveined
- 1 tablespoon olive oil
- 2 tablespoons lemon juice
- 1 tablespoon fresh parsley, chopped
- Salt and pepper to taste
- Wooden skewers (soaked in water for 30 minutes)

Instructions:

1. **Marinate the scallops and shrimp:**
   In a bowl, combine olive oil, lemon juice, parsley, salt, and pepper. Add the scallops and shrimp, tossing to coat. Let marinate for 15 minutes.
2. **Assemble the skewers:**
   Thread the scallops and shrimp onto the soaked skewers, alternating between the two.
3. **Grill the skewers:**
   Preheat the grill to medium-high heat. Grill the skewers for 2-3 minutes per side, or until the seafood is opaque and cooked through.
4. **Serve:**
   Serve the scallop and shrimp skewers with extra lemon wedges.

Lobster Tail with Garlic Butter

Ingredients:

- 2 lobster tails
- 4 tablespoons butter, melted
- 3 cloves garlic, minced
- 1 tablespoon fresh parsley, chopped
- 1 teaspoon lemon juice
- Salt and pepper to taste

Instructions:

1. **Prepare the lobster tails:**
   Using kitchen scissors, cut down the center of the lobster shells to expose the meat. Gently pull the meat out and rest it on top of the shell.
2. **Make the garlic butter:**
   In a small bowl, combine the melted butter, garlic, parsley, lemon juice, salt, and pepper.
3. **Cook the lobster tails:**
   Preheat the grill to medium-high heat. Brush the lobster meat with the garlic butter and grill for 5-7 minutes, basting with more butter halfway through, until the meat is opaque.
4. **Serve:**
   Serve the lobster tails with extra garlic butter on the side.

Tuna Melt

Ingredients:

- 1 can (5 oz) tuna, drained
- 2 tablespoons mayonnaise
- 1 tablespoon Dijon mustard
- 1 tablespoon fresh dill, chopped
- 2 slices whole wheat or white bread
- 2 slices cheddar cheese
- 1 tablespoon butter

Instructions:

1. **Prepare the tuna filling:**
   In a bowl, combine the tuna, mayonnaise, Dijon mustard, and dill. Season with salt and pepper.
2. **Assemble the sandwich:**
   Spread the tuna mixture on one slice of bread. Top with cheese, then place the second slice of bread on top.
3. **Grill the sandwich:**
   Heat butter in a skillet over medium heat. Grill the sandwich for 2-3 minutes per side, until golden brown and the cheese is melted.
4. **Serve:**
   Serve the tuna melt warm with a side of pickle chips.

Clam Bake

Ingredients:

- 2 dozen fresh clams, scrubbed
- 1 lb lobster tails, split in half
- 1 lb large shrimp, peeled and deveined
- 4 ears corn, husked and halved
- 1 lb small red potatoes, halved
- 1/2 cup melted butter
- 1 tablespoon Old Bay seasoning
- 2 lemons, cut into wedges
- Fresh parsley for garnish

Instructions:

1. **Prepare the ingredients:**
   Scrub the clams and split the lobster tails in half. Cut the corn and potatoes into halves.
2. **Cook the potatoes:**
   In a large pot, bring water to a boil and cook the potatoes for 10 minutes, or until slightly tender. Drain and set aside.
3. **Set up the bake:**
   In a large pot or Dutch oven, layer the corn, potatoes, clams, lobster tails, and shrimp. Pour the melted butter over everything and sprinkle with Old Bay seasoning.
4. **Steam the clams:**
   Cover the pot tightly and cook over medium heat for about 15-20 minutes, or until the clams open and the lobster and shrimp are cooked through.
5. **Serve:**
   Serve the clam bake with lemon wedges and fresh parsley for garnish.

Fish Casserole

Ingredients:

- 1 lb white fish fillets (such as cod or haddock)
- 1/2 cup sour cream
- 1/2 cup mayonnaise
- 1 cup shredded cheddar cheese
- 1/2 cup breadcrumbs
- 2 tablespoons butter, melted
- 1 teaspoon lemon juice
- 1/2 teaspoon garlic powder
- Salt and pepper to taste
- Fresh parsley for garnish

Instructions:

1. **Prepare the fish:**
   Preheat the oven to 375°F (190°C). Place the fish fillets in a greased baking dish. Season with salt, pepper, and garlic powder.
2. **Make the casserole topping:**
   In a small bowl, mix the sour cream, mayonnaise, cheddar cheese, breadcrumbs, melted butter, and lemon juice. Spread the mixture evenly over the fish fillets.
3. **Bake the casserole:**
   Bake in the preheated oven for 20-25 minutes, until the fish is cooked through and the topping is golden and bubbly.
4. **Serve:**
   Garnish with fresh parsley and serve hot with steamed vegetables or rice.

Lobster Ravioli

Ingredients:

- 1 lb fresh ravioli (store-bought or homemade)
- 1 lb lobster meat, cooked and chopped
- 1/2 cup ricotta cheese
- 1/4 cup grated Parmesan cheese
- 1 tablespoon fresh parsley, chopped
- 2 tablespoons olive oil
- 2 cloves garlic, minced
- 1/4 cup heavy cream
- 1/4 cup white wine
- 1 tablespoon lemon juice
- Salt and pepper to taste

Instructions:

1. **Make the ravioli filling:**
   In a bowl, combine the lobster meat, ricotta cheese, Parmesan, and parsley. Season with salt and pepper. Stuff the ravioli with this mixture.
2. **Cook the ravioli:**
   Boil the ravioli in salted water according to package instructions, usually 3-4 minutes, until they float to the surface.
3. **Make the sauce:**
   In a skillet, heat olive oil over medium heat. Add garlic and cook for 1 minute. Add the white wine, heavy cream, and lemon juice. Simmer for 5 minutes until the sauce thickens slightly.
4. **Combine and serve:**
   Toss the cooked ravioli in the sauce and serve hot with extra Parmesan on top.

Shrimp and Spinach Salad

Ingredients:

- 1 lb cooked shrimp, peeled and deveined
- 4 cups fresh spinach, washed
- 1/2 red onion, thinly sliced
- 1/2 cucumber, sliced
- 1/4 cup feta cheese, crumbled
- 1/4 cup olive oil
- 2 tablespoons balsamic vinegar
- 1 tablespoon Dijon mustard
- Salt and pepper to taste

Instructions:

1. **Prepare the salad:**
   In a large bowl, combine the spinach, shrimp, red onion, cucumber, and feta cheese.
2. **Make the dressing:**
   In a small bowl, whisk together olive oil, balsamic vinegar, Dijon mustard, salt, and pepper.
3. **Toss and serve:**
   Pour the dressing over the salad and toss gently to combine. Serve immediately.

Baked Tilapia with Lemon and Herbs

Ingredients:

- 4 tilapia fillets
- 2 tablespoons olive oil
- 1 lemon, sliced
- 2 garlic cloves, minced
- 1 teaspoon dried thyme
- 1 teaspoon dried rosemary
- Salt and pepper to taste
- Fresh parsley for garnish

Instructions:

1. **Prepare the fillets:**
   Preheat the oven to 375°F (190°C). Place the tilapia fillets on a baking sheet lined with parchment paper.
2. **Season the fish:**
   Drizzle the olive oil over the fillets. Sprinkle with garlic, thyme, rosemary, salt, and pepper. Top with lemon slices.
3. **Bake the tilapia:**
   Bake for 12-15 minutes, or until the fish flakes easily with a fork.
4. **Serve:**
   Garnish with fresh parsley and serve with your favorite side dish.

Crab and Corn Chowder

Ingredients:

- 1 lb crab meat, cooked and shredded
- 2 cups corn kernels (fresh or frozen)
- 1/2 cup diced onion
- 2 cloves garlic, minced
- 2 cups chicken or vegetable broth
- 2 cups half-and-half
- 2 tablespoons butter
- 2 medium potatoes, peeled and diced
- 1/4 cup fresh parsley, chopped
- Salt and pepper to taste

Instructions:

1. **Sauté the vegetables:**
   In a large pot, melt butter over medium heat. Add the onion and garlic and cook until softened, about 3 minutes.
2. **Add the potatoes and corn:**
   Add the diced potatoes and corn kernels to the pot. Stir in the chicken broth and bring to a boil. Reduce the heat and simmer for 10-12 minutes, or until the potatoes are tender.
3. **Make the chowder:**
   Add the half-and-half to the pot and bring to a simmer. Stir in the crab meat and cook for 5 minutes.
4. **Finish and serve:**
   Season with salt and pepper, then garnish with fresh parsley. Serve hot with crusty bread.

www.ingramcontent.com/pod-product-compliance
Lightning Source LLC
LaVergne TN
LVHW081341060526
838201LV00055B/2776